Hitler's

"Mein Kampf"

and the —

Present War

by
A. P. MAYVILLE

A CRITICAL SURVEY OF THE NAZI
BIBLE OF HATE AND ITS EFFECT ON
PRE-WAR EVENTS IN GERMANY FROM
WHICH EMANATED THE IMPENDING
CATACLYSM OF THE WORLD.

AMERICAN GOODWILL ASSOCIATION

Printing Statement:

Due to the very old age and scarcity of this book, many of the pages may be hard to read due to the blurring of the original text, possible missing pages, missing text and other issues beyond our control.

Because this is such an important and rare work, we believe it is best to reproduce this book regardless of its original condition.

Thank you for your understanding.

HITLER'S "MEIN KAMPF"

and the

PRESENT WAR

by

A. P. MAYVILLE

"There is nothing the rabble fears more than Intelligence. If they understood what is truly terrifying, they would fear ignorance.

—Goethe.

American Goodwill Association
Suite 50, 19 West 21st Street, New York, N. Y.

WHY THE WAR?

WHY ARE ALL those atrocities committed which devastate the civilized world at present? Whence came that consuming hatred between nations which is now engaging the flower of mankind in a deadly struggle? Why is the young blood of Europe now being shed in such unprecedented proportions? Why the ruthless air bombardments of peaceful cities and towns destroying women and children, the aged and disabled? Why the wanton destruction of priceless treasures and property which mankind has laboriously accumulated through the ages? Why should homes be filled with weeping mothers, wives and children, whose sons, husbands and fathers have been killed or crippled on the battlefields? Why have millions of children been torn from their homes and placed with strange people and in foreign surroundings?

There was not and there still is no reason for this war except that one crazed man—Adolf Hitler willed it.

The war, from its very beginning, is not, as many think, a struggle for the status of Danzig or some kind of an absurd Corridor, not even a struggle for the national existence of Poland or any other nation involved. There are bigger stakes involved. The war has now turned to purely ideological issues. It is Hitlerism versus the fundamental rights of man. It is brutal force versus tolerance; slavery versus freedom. It is whether the world should continue to tolerate the possibility of a one-man rule. In short, it is Hitler versus the world, barbarism versus civilization, the rule of the jungle versus humanitarian principles.

Who is this man Hitler? What are his teachings? His philosophy? His ruling system? A comprehensive answer to these questions are laid down by Hitler in his own book "Mein Kampf," which he wrote at the beginning of his political career. That book has since served as the Nazi profession of faith. The teachings of that book are followed by Hitler and his followers with a religious fervor. To understand the real reason for the present World War one must get an inside view of "Mein Kampf."

HITLER'S TESTAMENT OF HATE

MEIN KAMPF, Hitler's autobiography, is a most striking as well as a most disturbing exhibit of a pathological mind. While in ordinary times such a deposition would be of interest only to the professional alienist as a clinical record, it has now, tragically enough, become of vital concern to all of us.

He was never a pacifist, boasts Hitler, and he has always claimed that fight was the essence and flavor of life. He has firmly believed that "only people of brutal will-power will triumph and that mankind grew great in eternal battle, while in eternal peace it will go to destruction." He has, therefore, sought throughout his life opportunities for scrapping with some one. In his childhood he victimized his father at home and his teacher at school. By the time he reached maturity his feelings of hate over whelmed him completely. He hated everyone and everybody. He hated his king, he hated democracy, he hated alike his fellow workers and his employers; he hated law and order, and he was filled with joy wherever he saw destruction and whenever he heard of war.

War, war above everything, was his motto, and, rightly or wrongly,, "what is denied to amity the fist must take" . . War, proclaims he, should have no code of ethics; in wars even the most brutal acts are permissible. He was always convinced, that "no state has ever yet been founded by peaceful economy, but only by the instincts that preserve the species, whether they take the form of heroic virtue or *crafty cunning.*"

Even when he was still very young he used to "despair that he had been born into an age which evidently would build its temples of fame only for tradesmen or civil servants," and he would exclaim: *"Why could not I have been born a hundred years sooner? Say at the time of the Wars of Liberation, when a man really had some value, even apart from business."*

"I had been annoyed," writes Hitler, *"that my earthly journey was begun, as I thought, too late, and had regarded the age of 'peace and good order' ahead of me as an undeserved meanness of fate. For even as a boy I was no 'pacifist', and every attempt to train me in that direction was a fizzle."*

Therefore, he was extremely delighted when the World War broke out. To him "those days seemed like deliverance from the angry feelings of his youth." "I am not ashamed to say that even now," he relates, "that I fell on my knees, overcome by a storm of enthusiasm, and thanked heaven out of an overflowing heart that it had granted me the good fortune to live in this age."

Hitler, who prides himself so much on his militarism and his enthusiasm for warfare, was in the first World War in the German army six full years, claims to have been wounded twice, pretends to have participated in many a battle, and, yet, received no decoration and rose only to the rank of corporal in the army hierarchy.

It is obvious that Hitler is very good at preaching battle to his subjects, but personally he dodged battle when he was in the army, and his superiors could find nothing in him to justify distinction. To be promoted in the army one has to be both intelligent and daring, and Hitler possessed neither of these qualities. His only distinctions are hooliganism and cowardice, as this extraordinary autobiography amply reveals. *Mein Kampf*, written in an atrocious style, is full of misstatements and lies and countless contradictions. It discloses the psychology of the underworld and gangsterism. By its methods Hitler could appeal to the lowliest instincts of the uneducated and deluded German masses, but these did not serve him to good purpose in gaining higher military rank.

Hitler looks with disfavor at culture. For gangsterism culture is useless and at times it may even be dangerous. Lack of culture serves it to far better advantage. Hitler acknowledges it quite explicitly and he says: *One thing all the ink-stained knights and fools of today should take particularly to heart: the great upheavals in this world have never been guided by a goose-quill.*

— 4 —

"Ink-stained knights and fools" — this is the best Hitler can find to say about men of culture, and he adds: *All great movements are people's movements; they are volcanic eruptions of human passions, set off either by the cruel Goddess of Privation or by the torch of words hurled among the masses. They are not the lemonade outpouring of aesthetic-talking literati and parlor heroes.*

Poor Germany! Her *Kultur* was her pride, and here comes an almost illiterate painter from Austria, a hoodlum from the underworld, ruthlessly striking at her foundations. Is it not a most cruel irony of fate, that what was so painstakingly built up during the ages by a Schiller, a Goethe, a Beethoven, a Kant, has now been laid waste by the insane demagogy of a megalomaniac.

Only due to the fact that the reactionary, chauvinistic, revengeful junkers and militarists of Germany were in need of a forgotten man, scraped up from the pit, for the purpose of heading its struggle against democracy and social reforms, was Hitler lifted up to power and ;lory. Without their fear for the imminent "danger" of liberal reforms in the German social and economic structure, Hitler could have stood no :hance whatsoever. An ignorant, wretched ex-painter, a broken, wounded corporal became the demand of the hour. He was the best qualified of all the potential candidates. Being a good orator he could inflame the masses. Being ill-cultured he could talk absurdities with the full pathos of conviction, and crazed by hatred he carried promise of crushing all their foes.

Hitler was and still is a mere tool in the hands of the world reactionaries. Spain needed a Franco. Reactionary retrogressive Italy demanded a Mussolini. The junkers and money bags of Germany placed an order for a *Lumpenproletarier* — and the order was filled.

Hitler played his role magnificently. True to the code of morals of the underworld, wherefrom he sprang to leadership, he is opposed to any humanitarian or aesthetical conceptions, which are, as he eloquently expresses his thoughts, "but inventions of the 'lowliest of mankind,' the Jews and their provocative agencies (suggesting the Church of Christ), which preaches the gospels of love and justice to lead mankind to its destruction." *"When people fight,"* is his gospel, *"all considerations of humaneness or aesthetics crumble into nothing; for these conceptions are not floating in the ether of the world, but are born of man's imagination, and are bound to it. His departure from this world dissolves those concepts into nothing again, for Nature knows them not."* Therefore, he adds, *"the cruelest weapons were humane if they brought quicker victory, and only those methods were beautiful which helped assure the dignity of freedom for the nation."*

So away with you, "aesthetic, sickly apes!" — pacifists of all kinds and all nations.

No doubt, Hitler is a skilled social spider who expertly weaves the cobwebs around his victims. Under favorable conditions, the victim is found in close proximity and he offers very little resistance. Whether an individual or a country, he will soon be enmeshed in the cobwebs of Goebbels-Hitler propaganda. Hitler is very far from the democratic ideals of our time, the concern of which is never propaganda, but enlightenment, honest criticism and rationalism. In his Nazism Hitler is but a loyal son of the 19th century's reaction against republicanism, which has sought to revive the carcass of racialism-nationalism of the pre-Christian era the aim of which was to combat the French Revolution. Militarized junker-Germany, which the Kaiser subjugated and tamed by Nationalism versus Cosmopolitanism-Republicanism, decided to use against its own Republic and its trend for social reforms the very same chauvinistic *nationalism*, which lead towards its defeat in the first World War.

Nationalism, in its chauvinistic aspect, has always been an implement of reaction, unless it arose to forestall the still greater evil, — racialism or tribalism, based on consanguinity the origin of which dates back to the Totem period. The latter is both in essence and substance the very doctrine that Hitler has decided to preach through his Nazism.

It is very easy to befog simple brains. But how long can muddleheadedness remain in saddle? There is a time-limit set for machinations of this kind, for their maintenance demands a constant, superhuman effort.

What if the masses open their eyes? All will be finished. Sheer brutal force will never be made a normal basis of any society for very long. *The masses*, says Hitler, *have no inkling of the whole doctrine's inward error. They see only the ruthless strength and brutality of its expression, which eventually they always yield to.*

To stir the masses, not to enlighten them, is the role of any racialist hero. But this method requires administering doses of increasing potency. And Hitler relates about himself: *I knew the nature of the broad masses well enough to realize that 'aesthetic' loftiness was no way to keep the flames necessary to keep the iron hot.* And further: *The great masses' capacity to absorb is very limited, their understanding small, and their forgetfulness is great. For these reasons any effective propaganda must be confined to a very few points, and must use these as slogans until the very last man cannot help knowing what is meant. The moment we give up this principle, and try to vary things, we dissipate our effect, since the crowd can neither digest nor retain what we offer it. This again weakens and finally destroys the results.*

For this reason Hitler began his search for an adequate slogan. The theory was furnished by Germany of the 19th century which vanquished the humanitarian France of the 18th century, — the practice was handed to Hitler by the shortsightedness of the makers of the Treaty of Versailles: a defeated, degraded, plundered Germany, a Germany of reparations and humiliations. To become a liberator, to restore Germany was an expedient camouflage for driving out democracy, for crushing the labor movement, for abolishing parliament and social reforms. The Fatherland is humbled, the Nation is in dust, the heart of the German people is stabbed, the blood is gushing, therefore,— down with class and individual, down with liberties, down with trade unions, workers' aspirations, ideals! Down with democracies, freedom, when great Germany is under the heel of the allies and is crucified by the shameless Treaty of Versailles!

Thus was born *Mein Kampf*.

But all that, thought Hitler, was too much for the masses to grasp. He knew, that "the intelligence of the common people is of limited capacity," and the blunders of the Treaty of Versailles were too complicated to be of direct concern to arouse the masses. A more simple slogan had to be unearthed. He looked for one and found it: *The Jew!*

It did not matter to him that he did not know who and what the Jews were. It is not the truth that he was after, but the scapegoat, the prey for the beast. So let it be the Jew! Thus he began to introduce the Jew as the embodiment of everything that he conceived evil in the world. Who caused the poverty of the German masses? The Jews. Who brought about Germany's defeat in the World-War? The Jews. The Jews dominate both the White House in Washington and the Krmelin in Moscow. They are the International Bankers who fight labor and they are the Marxists who fight the International Bankers. They are democracy and dictatorship. They are war and peace. In short, they are the magic lamp that can be used for all purposes of propaganda.

In this game what matter lies and contradiction? It is sufficient that an easy prey is at hand to quench his sadistic thirst for blood. The Jews are within easy reach and are defenseless. In his innermost soul Hitler is reaching out for bigger game. His craving for blood can be satisfied with nothing lass than the present slaughter of world-wide magnitude. But this he then reserved for the present days when Germany became thoroughly re-militarized. For that time the Jews sufficed.

"TRINKEN FRANZOSENBLUT"

HITLER'S father was a petty civil servant. He wished his son to prepare himself for the same career, and the first training he wanted to give him was a lesson in submissiveness; but the son rose against his father in revolt. He was found to possess some capacity for drawing and he, therefore, obstinately persisted in his aspirations to become a painter. It was not that he felt an inclination toward painting. His father was against it, and this decided the issue. Hitler, with all his rise to glory, remained a tragic figure for himself and for the world. As one of the down-trodden and simple mind-ed whose brain is not illuminated by an ideal of future abundance, of aboli-tion of poverty and suffering, Hitler was embittered against the world. Therefore, though his book, *Mein Kampf*, extends over 600 pages, there is not one ray of hope, of ultimate tri-umph of the good, of abolition of evil and oppression; nor can one find there even a single spark of love emanating from a heart which knew loving kind-ness and which has suffered, if not for all mankind, at least for some one other than himself.

Did some one ever caress Hitler? Did some one ever love him? This type of man was made to ever "obey orders," to be forever an underling of underlings. In the army, too, he was the Forgotten Man, the under-dog to whom any superior could mete out any indignity, on whom anyone could wipe his unclean hands as with a towel. A spirit of enmity against the hostile world often arises in such a damned soul, and if by some extraordinary miracle or treacherous mercy it should subsequently reach power, it, in turn, damns everybody whom it touches. The deadening tedium of such dejected life might express itself, as in the case of Hitler, in finding compensative delight in being cruel to the point of insanity. And insane, truly, he is.

In school his favorite subject was history, which in old textbooks was only a history of war, not that of human achievement. Metternich's Aus-tria was one of the masters of the "Holy Alliance" which restored the monarchy in Spain just as the present Axis restored their dictatorship.

Austria of the Hapsburgs was incomparably more conservative than Germany of the Kaisers; it was a bureaucratic Germany without the German genius. Hitler, like all Austrian children, was victimized by the monarchist · anti-republican propaganda, which was poisoning the schoolchildren's minds with false purposive hatred for the French. Therefore the children's theatrical plays abounded with songs the refrains of which read: "Trinken Franzosenblut" ("To Drink French Blood"), which really meant Republican blood. It was the same hatred for republican principles that led the Kaiser to bring about the drowning of American passenger boats with such a cynical delight. It was again *Trinken Franzosenblut.*

Little wonder that Hitler was brought up on that monarchical substitution of "French" blood for "Republican" blood.

Hitler grew up among brother and sisters, without, however, recognizing family ties. Not a single time does he mention them in his book. The feeling of love is so foreign to him that not even his closest relatives and friends did he ever cherish.

What may be the cause of his misanthropy? The direct psychological cause of it may lie in his bachelorhood. He is physically unfit for married life. He, therefore, hates women, and the misogeny of common bachelors sometimes passes also into a misandry. a hatred of the male. Such, it might appear, is the case with Hitler.

HITLER'S DEVELOPMENT FROM A SCAB TO AN INTERNATIONAL GANGSTER

HITLER was born in the town of Braunn in Austria, not far from the German border. His parents died very young, without bequeathing him anything. Hitler started out for Vienna in search of a livelihood. There began his real struggle for existence.

He went about looking for an occupation, but he did not succeed very much. In his native town he was considered a good designer. But when he had shown his drawings, he was advised to become an architect. When he wanted to take up architecture, he was given to understand that he would do better to stick to painting . . .

In his misery Hitler was thrown into the midst of the despised and the down trodden. Unfortunately some of these wretched, not enlightened by a higher vision and guided by blind emotion rather than reason, wander into submersive movements. In Hitler's case it was chauvinistic Nationalism, which spells extreme hatred to everything foreign.

The trade union movement of Vienna in those days was cosmopolitan. Hitler, therefore, was opposed to it even to the extent of "scabbing".

He confesses it shamelessly. On one of his jobs, he relates, *he met with a pestilence masquerading as social virtue and love of one's neighbor, a pestilence from which humanity must soon free the earth, lest the earth soon be freed of humanity.*

The pestilence in question is the trade union, which he was asked to join. *But, he confesses, his knowledge of the trade-union organization at that time was zero. He could have proved neither its usefulness nor its uselessness. As he was told he must*

— 8 —

join, he refused. He gave as his reason that he did not understand the situation, but would not be forced to do anything whatever. Perhaps the former was the motive why they did not throw him out at once. They must have hoped they could convert him or wear him down within a few days. In any case they were deeply mistaken. But within a fortnight he had reached the end of his ability, even if he had wanted to go on. In that fortnight he came to know his surroundings better, so that no power in the world could have forced him to join the trade union.

The consequences were quite natural. He was forced either to leave the job at once or to fly off the scaffolding on his head. As he was alone, he confesses, and resistance seemed hopeless, he preferred to follow the former advice, richer by one experience.

He would rather be jobless than to join the trade union. He left the scaffolding, *filled with disgust, but at the same time so agitated that it would have been quite impossible for him to turn his back on the whole affair. No; after the flaming up of the first indignation, his stiff neck once more got the upper hand. He.was absolutely determined to find another construction job just the same. His decision was strengthened by the privation which closed him in its heartless embrace a few weeks later, after he had eaten up what little wages he had saved. Now he had to, whether or no. And the game began all over again, only to end as it had before.*

Having met with these unpleasant experiences he began to study the character of the trade unions. He was told that they were dominated by the Socialists. Hence he was initiated into hating Marxism. Amongst the leaders of the Socialist movement in Austria he met with a few names of foreign origin, especially those of Jews, hence the beginning of his animosity for every non-German in general, and for every Jew in particular.

Austria was an empire of many nationalities with only ten million Germans and forty million other nationals, such as Czechs, Magyars, Croats, Serbs, Poles, Slovaks, Jews, and Hitler was utterly enraged when he saw the latter nationalities enjoying equal rights with the former. He even began hating the Hapsburg dynasty for its tolerance of the non-Germans and he exclaimed in his anguish: *Who, finally, could still preserve his allegiance to the emperors of a dynasty which had betrayed the interests of the German people again and again for its own petty advantage?*

In what consists that "betrayal"? whoever has ears let him hear:

In the north and in the south the poison of foreign peoples ate into the body of Austria, and even Vienna was obviously becoming more and more an un-German city. The House of the Archdukes favored Czechs wherever possible; it was the hand of the goddess of eternal justice and implacable retribution that overthrew the deadliest enemy of Austrian Germanity, Archduke Francis Ferdinand by the very bullets he had helped to cast. After all, he was the patron and protector of the attempt to slavicize Austria from above.

Hitler is known as an anti-Semite. But his anti-Semitism is only a part of his general animosity for everything and everybody. As a preacher of war, he could not but hate Germans, too. How many "pure" Germans were slaughtered by him in Concentration Camps, nobody knows. And how many Germans will now be slaughtered on the battlefields only history will tell. Until his advent Germany had never preached the cult of racialism. It is, as a matter of fact, contradictory to the true enlightened German spirit. Rutzel's classic study in anthropology, "Voelkerkunde," contradicts Hitler's faked up racialism. Why then does Mein Kampf abound with so many passages in which Hitler reviles all other nationalities?

We have our suspicions about the sincerity of these utterances. All this is sheer demagogy calculated to work on the mind of the German Massenmensch, to capture him by flattery and to endow him with immunity against class-consciousness. As a matter of fact, it has been proven that at the time Hitler was clamoring for his nationals of Sudetenland or of Danzig, he sacrificed the Germans of Tyrol to political expedience. By this act he demonstrated that his racial theory is also a mere expedient, discarded as soon as the purpose is served.

The closest neighbors of Germany are the Slavs. Hitler has set his mind on conquering and enslaving them eventually as he has done to the Czechs and Slovaks. He has prepared the ground for these actions by filling many pages of Mein Kampf with utterances of animosity towards them, by claiming that the preservative force of Slavism is highly doubtful, and thereby admitting that if European soil was wanted, by and large, it could be had only at the expense of Russia; the new Empire must have returned to march the road of the ancient Knights of the German Order, to give soil to the German plow . . . by the German sword, and to win the daily bread of the nation . . .

He hates the Slavs to such an extent that he places in disrepute even Austria for its alliance with those nations, claiming that, as a matter of race policy, the alliance of Germany with Austria was simply "ruinous!" The growth was tolerated of a new great Slavic power, Austria, on the borders of the Empire; therefore he rejoiced in the defeat of the Russians (in the Russo-Japanese war) because he saw in it at the same time a defeat of the Austrian Slavs.

In Pan-German circles of those times, one heard the opinion that Austrian Germanity might well succeed in Germanizing the Austrian Slavs, but in Hitler's opinion, they never realised for a moment, that Germanization can be applied only to soil, never to people.

What was generally understood by this word, in his conception, a forced outward acceptance of the German language; but it is an almost inconceivable error to believe that, for instance, a Negro or a Chinese becomes a Teuton because he learns German and is ready to speak the German language in the future, and perhaps to give his vote to a German political party . . .

For if the forcible imposition of a common language today bridges and finally wipes out previously conspicuous differences between various peoples, this is the beginning of bastardization, and thus in this case not a Germanization but a destruction of that Germanic element.

Therefore, he rejoiced, that the Germanization of Austria in the sense of Joseph II never took place; its result would have been the survival of the Austrian State, but also a lowering of the racial level of the German nation- produced by the community of language; in the course of centuries a certain herd instinct would probably have crystallized, but the herd itself would have been inferior; a people constituting a state might have been born, but a civilizing people would have been lost . . . It was better for the German nation that this process of mixing remained unaccomplished, even though it was not due to any noble insight, but to the "narrow short-sightedness" of the Hapsburgs; had it been otherwise, the German people could no longer be described as a cultural factor.

He found "revolting" the conglomeration of races which the Imperial capital (Vienna) presented, "revolting" the whole mixture of Czechs, Poles, Hungarians, Ruthenians, Serbs and Croatians, etc.; and to him the gigantic city seemed the "embodiment of incest". The German of his youth, he tells, was the dialect which is spoken also in Lower Bavaria; he could neither forget it nor learn the Viennese "jargon". The longer he stayed in the city, the higher burned his hatred for the "alien admixture of peoples" which began to "gnaw away" at this ancient seat of German culture. Then he left Vienna, as he says, in disgust, and he was overjoyed to see Munich — "A German city". What a difference after Vienna, said he, "Even to think back on that 'Babylon of races' turned his stomach."

Not alone the Slavs, the French,

too, are the arch-enemies of the German people, and it is his (Hitler's) "holy mission" to destroy them. Why? because "France remains by far the most terrible enemy of Germany. This nation, which is being permeated more and more with negro blood, represents a lurking danger to the existence of the white race in Europe."

Hitler believes Bismarck to have been the greatest statesman of Germany whose work, however, was not completed, because he left the question of Alsace Lorraine half solved: Instead of brutally crushing the head of the French hydra once and for all, and then giving equal rights to the Alsatian, he did neither.

What Bismarck has failed to accomplish Germany must do now: About this finally one must be perfectly clear: France is and remains the inexorable enemy of the German people. And he exults: The French race which is gradually dying out, not only in respect to the size of her population, but more so in regard to her best racial elements . . .

This is due to the fact, that the French, thinks Hitler, mix their blood with the blood of negroes . . .

SCIENTIFIC FACTS ABOUT RACE AND HITLER'S IGNORANCE

RACE . . . Blood . . . Purity of Blood . . . Defilement of Blood . . . Only the Germans were chosen by the Almighty to perfect His Creation. They are the only ones whose blood is pure. They are the only bearers of culture. All the other nations of the world may be tolerated only to the extent of their rendering service to the German cause . . .

Let us be clear about it. What are the real scientific facts about Race? On that let us quote the world-famous authority on anthropology,

Professor Franz Boaz of the Department of Anthropology of the Columbia University, who declares that:

Even the most in-bred population consists of family lines of different character. Yet local groups of the white race are so much alike that the extremes of one type are much more dissimilar than the averages of any two types.

The claim that racial descent determines behavior nowadays rests upon a misapplication under which racial type and behavior are being considered as two aspects of the same phenomenon without investigation of how far the two are related.

The posture and gestures which have been claimed to be racially determined depend upon environment and in the United States change from those of immigrants to those of their American descendants. The types of crimes committed differ in character and frequency from those committed by their descendants whose crime records are quite similar to those of native-born Americans.

In order to better explain these scientific facts Prof. Boaz refers to Mayor La Guardia of New York:

"Mayor La Guardia, speaking English to Americans uses American gestures; speaking Italian to Italians, he uses Italian gestures."

Discussing what he termed "the incredible amount of amateurish work produced for more than a century" by "modern race enthusiasts," Professor Boaz said:

According to our familiarity with bodily forms found in various localities, we are apt to establish these as definite concepts according to which we classify the great variety of human forms. We pursue the same process in the classification of our general experiences, which always depend upon the character of our previous impressions and only to a lesser extent upon objective characteristics. The naive classification of human types does not represent a grouping according to biological principles, but is based on individual experience.

Discussing world types, Professor Boaz said:

We must bear in mind that groups impressing us as a conglomerate of different conceptualized types may actually be of common descent, and that others appearing to us as representatives of one type may include groups of distinct origin.

To blast the very foundation of Hitler's race theory, thereby demolishing the entire basis upon which the Nazi state has been built, a statement was recently issued by the Society for the Psychological Study of Social Issues, and was signed by the outstanding psychologists in the American universities.

The statement is partly as follows:

The Fascists and many others have grossly misused the term "Race". According to anthropoligists, the term "Race" may legitimately be used only for such groups as possess in common certain physical or bodily characteristics which distinguish them from other groups. It is impossible to speak correctly of a "German Race" or of an "Italian Race" since both of these groups have highly diversified bodily characteristics. A South German may resemble a Frenchman from Auvergne or an Italian from Piedmont more closely than he does a German from Hanover. North Italians are markedly dissimilar from those living in Sicily or Naples. More important still, the emphasis on the existence of an "Aryan Race" has no scientific basis, since the word "Aryan" refers to a family of languages and not at all to race or to physical appearance. As far as the Jews are concerned, scientific investigations have shown them to be tall or short, blond or dark, round-headed or long-headed, according to the particular community studied. In the light of this wide variation in physical characteristics, almost all anthropoligists outside of Germany and Italy would agree that it is scientifically impossible to speak of a "Jewish race", much less of an "Aryan Race."

In the experiments which psychologists have made upon different peoples, no characteristic, inherent psychological differences which fundamentally distinguish so-called "races" have been disclosed. There is no evidence for the existence of an inborn Jewish or German or Italian mentality. Furthermore, there is no indication that the members of any group are rendered incapable by their biological heredity of completely acquiring the culture of the community in which they live. This is true not only of the Jews in Germany, but also of groups that actually are physically different from one another. The Nazi theory that people must be related by blood in order to participate in the same cultural or intellectual heritage has absolutely no support from scientific findings ... Racial and national attitudes are psychologically complex, and cannot be understood except in terms of their economic, political and historical backgrounds. Psychologists find no basis for the explanation of such attitudes in terms of innate mental differences between racial and national groups. The many attempts to establish such differences have so far met failure. Even if successful they would offer no justification for repressive treatment of the type now current in Germany. In the scientific investigations of human groups by psychologists, no conclusive evidence has been found for racial or national differences in native intelligence and inherited personality characteristics. Certainly no individual should be treated as an inferior merely because of his membership in one human group rather than another. Here in America, we have clear indication of the manner in which members of different racial and national groups have combined to create a common culture.

But Hitler is a man who is neither able nor willing to reckon with scientific facts. He is a bigot parading as a scientist and uses the concept race as a mask with which to cloak cruelty and to justify sadistic inclinations. He has heard something about Darwinism, Evolution, and "Survival of the fittest"; in addition he must have heard something about Nietzsche's idea of the "Superman." To digest it properly he was, naturally, incapable and he enmeshed all of it in a theory which is absurd to the point that it would be ludicrous if it did not spell the tragedy of millions of deluded German people, who accepted his theory as if it were the dictate of fate, and are now paying for it with their lives.

"Nationality, or rather race, is not in language, but in blood," is Hitler's given law for the German, and he continues: *and so it could be possible to speak of Germanization only if this process succeeded in transforming the blood of the inferior; but this is impossible; a mingling of blood might produce a change, but it would mean the depression of the level of the superior race; the final result of such a process, that is, would be the destruction of those very qualities which once made victory possible for the conquering people; cultural powers in particular would disappear on mating with a lower race, even though the resulting mongrels spoke the language of the former superior race a thousand times over; for a time there will be some struggle between the differing spirits; it may be that the declining people, in a sort of last spurt, produces surprising cultural assets; but these are only single elements belonging to the higher race, or bastards of the first generation in*

— 13 —

whom the better blood still predominates and strives to break through; they are never the ultimate products of the mixture; these will always exhibit a culturally retrogressive motion.

All these he mentions by way of his disapproval of the equality of rights that was granted to the Slavs in the old Austrian domain, and he adds: *not only in Austria, but in Germany itself so-called Nationalist circles are influenced by similar false reasoning; the oft-demanded policy of Germanizing the Polish East unfortunately almost always rested on the same fallacy; they believed the Polish element could be Germanized by a purely linguistic process of Teutonization. Here, too, the result would have been disastrous—a people of alien race expressing its alien thoughts in the German language, comprising the exaltation and dignity of our nationality by its own inferiority.*

Then he intones: *Historically, the thing usefully Germanized has been the soil that was conquered with the sword, and settled with German peasants; in so far as alien blood was introduced into the body of the German people they assisted in that pernicious disjunction which takes effect in German hyper-individualism — a quality unfortunately often actually praised.*

In short: here is the implication of the reasons, given by Hitler, why Germany should be militarized, why she should wage wars, annex territories and enslave other nations. "The basic conclusion," says Hitler, "is *that the state is not an end, but a means. It is indeed indispensable to the formation of higher human civilization, but it is not the cause; the latter consists exclusively in the existence of a race capable of culture; there might be hundreds of model states on earth, but if the German bearers of civiliza-*

tion were to die out no culture would exist that would correspond with the intellectual level of the most advanced peoples of today; the fact of the formation of human states by no means excludes the possibility of the destruction of the human race if superior intellectual ability and elasticity are lost, owing to the disappearance of their racial possessor;

If the surface of the earth were distributed today by some event, and a new Himalaya range were to rise from the ocean, the civilization of mankind would be destroyed in one cruel catastrophe; yet if from this chaos of horror but a few men of a definite race capable of civilization had escaped, the earth would once more show signs of human, creative power; only the destruction of the last civilizing race and its individual members would permanently devastate the earth; that state structures in their tribal beginnings cannot protect their racial members from destruction if the latter are lacking in capacity; just as certain species of great prehistoric animals were forced to give way to others, and altogether disappeared, so man must give way if he lacks a certain intellectual strength through which alone he can find the weapons necessary for his self-preservation;

The state does not in itself create a definite cultural level; it can only preserve the race which does so; otherwise the state as such may go on existing evenly for centuries, while, as a result of a mixture of races which it has not prevented, the cultural capacity and the resulting general life-pattern of a people have long since suffered profound change; the present-day state, for instance, may still simulate existence as a formal mechanism for a considerable length of time, but the racial poisoning of

— 14 —

the body produces a cultural decline which is already apparent;

Thus the existence of a higher humanity depends not on the State, but on the nationality capable of creating it.

What is that "Higher Humanity"? Hitler repeats it over and over again: Germany! "Deutschland, Deutschland, ueber Alles!" Only Germans and nobody else are chosen by the Almighty to lead — nay, — to rule the world, to purge it of its impurities, i. e., to annihilate that part of its population which bears the stigma of being born to any other but the Germanic race — because, says Hitler, *in a bastardized and negroid world, any concept of the humanly beautiful and noble as well as any image of an idealized future for humanity would be lost forever.*

Human culture and civilization on this continent are inseparable from the existence of the German; his extinction or downfall would once more drop the dark veil of uncivilized ages upon the globe;

In the eyes of any populist world-concept the undermining of the existence of human culture by destroying its sustainers, i. e., the Germans, is the most abhorrent of crimes; he who dares to lay his hand upon the highest likeness of the Lord offends against the good Creator of this miracle, and assists in the expulsion from Paradise.

Lest someone may come and point out the fact that the German civilization is of a comparatively recent date and that there were many civilizations prior to the German appearance on the historical arena of mankind, Hitler has an excuse ready: *it is an unbelievable outrage to represent the Teutons of pre-Christian times as "uncivilized", as barbarians. This they never were. The harshness of their Northern home merely forced*

conditions on them that prevented the development of their creative powers.

Friendship is meaningless to Hitler. With Italy he concluded an "Axis" pact of friendship and mutual support. Still, in his book, he heaps upon these allies a mountain of abuse: "Bastardized, Negroid cauldron of impurity, the Latin race;" while at his second "Axis" partner, Japan, he pours the full tide of one of his eloquent tirades, which can be summarized as follows:

It is not true, as many people suppose, that Japan is superimposing German technical progress on her own civilization; European science and technology are being embellished with Japanese style. The basis of real life is no longer a specially Japanese civilization, although that does set the color of life (which owing to the inner difference, is more outwardly conspicuous to the European), but the tremendous scientific and technical work of Europe and America, that is of German peoples. Only on the basis of these achievements can Japan follow general human progress. It is the basis of the struggle for daily bread; it forges the weapons and tools. Only the outward dress is gradually accommodated to Japanese character. If, starting today, all further German influence on Japan were to cease, supposing Germany to be destroyed, Japan's present advance in science and technology might continue for a while; but within a few years the well would run dry, the Japanese individuality would gain, but the present civilization would stiffen, and would sink back into the lethargy from which it was released seven decades ago by the wave of German civilization. And just as the present Japanese development owes its life to a German source, so once in the dim past an alien influence and an alien

— 15 —

HOW REALLY CULTURED GERMANY IS

IF HITLER were reasonable he would have thought twice before he had passed judgment on the abilities of any group of people to create cultural values. The process of negation may be quite successfully reversed, and in the light of his avowal of Germany's superiority and his insistent demand that the world recognize her primacy, one may claim the right to know how really great she is.

That Germany has given the world outstanding composers of music is irrefutable. In this field she is able to muster a roster that commands respect and admiration.

But it is a strange coincidence, that at the very time when Hitler was writing *Mein Kampf,* complimenting the Jewish people by such titular names, as "decomposing fungi of mankind", two Jews, Mischa Elman and Yasha Heifetz, were sensationally successful in Germany with their musical performances of compositions by the Jews; Mendelsohn, Halevi, and Maierbeer. At the same time the German Theatre was being uplifted in a revolutionary manner by . . . the Jew Max Reinhart.

Hitler pretends to be a painter of talent, and, therefore, summarizing art, he classifies painting as "the most noble of arts", and, is it not a cruel irony of fate, that at the time Hitler was, in his book, denouncing the Jew as incapable of any considerable achievement in that field of art, the presidency of the German Academy of Art was being bestowed upon . . . the Jew Max Liebermann.

In literature Germany has but three authors, whose works have attained the status of classics. They are: Goethe, Schiller, and . . . the Jew Heine. Germany has no writers to offer comparable to England's Shakespeare, Milton, Scott or Dickens; to Italy's Dante; to Spain's Cervantes; to France's Moliere, Dumas, Hugo or Maupassant; to Russia's Dostoievsky and Tolstoi.

However, amongst the modern writers there are several Germans who have acquired international fame. They are:

Jacob Wasserman, the two brothers Zweig, Ernest Toller, L. Feuchtwanger, Franz Werfel, and Thomas Mann, — seven in all. Now six of them are to be discounted, because . . . they are Jews. The seventh, Thomas Mann, has abjured his Fatherland bewailing her barbarous state under the savage regime of the Nazis.

Germany has given birth to philosophers like Kant, Nietzsche, Schopenhauer and Hegel. Their works, however, are so heavy and ponderous in style and text that they are difficult to read and comprehend. In fact, the works of Kant were a matter of speculation even among the most erudite Germans, until they were elucidated by the . . . Jew Herman Cohen. Moreover, Germany has no philosopher comparable to the Jew Spinoza.

Nor can Germany boast of having contributed a single outstanding electrical invention. The best she has has been able to do was to build upon the foundations laid by others. Al-

— 16 —

though her laboratories had access to world knowledge, the credit for the invention of the telegraph, the telephone, the cable, the dynamo, the electric light and a host of other electrical inventions must be given to others than Germans.

In medicine one expects Germany to have made numerous contributions of the first magnitude, but here, too, the loud mouthings of Hitler cannot maintain that this was accomplished without Jewish assistance. Jews born in Germany have made the most notable contributions to medicine overshadowing their "Aryan" colleagues

In connection with the Germans contribution to medicine I will note here the contents of an anonymous satirical leaflet, which is being passed around in New York :

MEDICAL INSTRUCTIONS — FOR NAZIS

Since it is imperative that all loyal Nazis avoid any and all contacts with Jewish influences, the following instructions, issued by order of Adolf Hitler, must be strictly followed:

A Nazi who has syphilis must not allow himself to be cured by salvarsan, because it was discovered by the Jew, Erlich. He must not even take steps to find out whether he has syphilis, because the Wasserman reaction, which is used for that purpose, is also the discovery of a Jew.

If a Nazi suspects that he has gonorrhea, he must not seek to establish the fact, because he will be using the method of a Jew, Neiser.

A Nazi who has heart disease must not use digitalis, which comes from the Jew, Ludwig Traube. If he has a toothache, a Nazi will not use cocaine, nor will he benefit by the work of a Jew, Solomon Stricker. Nor will he be treated for typhoid fever, or will have to benefit by the work and discoveries of the Jews, Widal and Weill.

If a Nazi has diabetes, he must not use insulin, because of the research work of a Jew, Minkowsky. If he has a headache, he must shun pyramidon and antipyrin, because of the Jews, Spiro and Eilege. Nazis with convulsions must put up with them.

because it was a Jew, Oscar Leibreich, who thought of chloral-hydrate. They must do likewise with their psychic ailments, because Freud, the father of Psychoanalysis, is also a Jew.

In short, a good loyal Nazi may fittingly and properly remain afflicted with syphilis, gonorrhea, heart disease, toothache, typhoid fever, diabetes, convulsions and mental disorders.

Nazi physicians must discard discoveries and improvements of the Nobel prize men — Volitzer, Barangaj, and Otto Warburg; of the dermatologists, Judassohn, Bruno, Block and Unna; of the neurologists, Mendi, Oppenheim, Kronecker, and Benedickt; of the lung specialist, Fraenkel; of the surgeon, Israel; of the anatomist, Henle; and of many such other Jewish scientists and medical experts.

This satire tells the whole story in a nutshell.

Indeed, there is not a single field in the many branches of human cultural achievements where one can claim German superiority.

Has Germany produced humanitarians as great as Tolstoi and Ghandi' Or Saints as St. Francis of Assissi'

Spiritual leaders as Moses, Buddha or Confucius?

There are about 100 million Germans; there are only 16 million Jews. Hitler considers the Jews as the "decomposing fungi of mankind". But can he claim for the Germans as many and as great contributors towards the civilization of mankind as the Jews can?

The teachings of God — Moses, the Prophets and the Saviour.

Rulers — King Solomon;

Philosophy — Maimonides, Crescas and Spinoza;

Poetry — Heinrich Heine;

Statesmen — Lord Beaconsfield;

Orators — Ferdinand Lassale;

Political Economy — Karl Marx;

Psychologists — Lombrozo and Freud;

Physics and Mathematics — Albert Einstein;

Men of Letters — Georg Brandes, and Emil Ludwig.

A WORD OF TIMELY WARNING

ALL THIS discourse was brought here not for the sake of claiming superiority or inferiority for any nation on earth, but to prove the absurdity of such contentions. Human culture is indivisible. Great men and great achievements are not the explicit possession of the nations who bore them, but belong to mankind in general. The Jews, for instance cannot lay any more claim to the Bible than other nations. The same may apply to Shakespeare, or Goethe, or Beethoven, or Einstein. Still, a word of timely warning is here in place, namely:

History fails to reveal a single nation which retained a supremacy based on cruelty, oppression, persecution and slaughter. Yet it is with this formula that Nazi Germany aspires to world greatness.

Gratitude and loyalty one marvels at in beasts but expects in man. The German Jews have served loyally their Fatherland even unto death. Over 12,000 Jews laid down their lives for the German cause in the first World War. In proportion to their population their sacrifices were overwhelming. As a matter of routine their names were inscribed on various monuments as Germans who died in defense of their country. The present authorities had these names erased. If such acts of barbarity are inherent in the entire German people, then not only the Jews, but every other nation in close proximity to the Reich stands in danger of being treated some day in the same manner. But not so! The German nation is as innocent of such barbarities as Hitler is guilty. Some day they will surely awaken and realize the truth. On that day they will be admitted once again to the civilized society of nations. Pray to God that it may not be too late in coming, lest the world will be in ruins, beyond redemption.

A DISTORTED GERMANY UNDER THE NAZI REGIME

THE REAL TRAGEDY of our time is the belief of millions of simple-minded Germans that "Mein Kampf," that curious demagogy of an unbalanced mind, to be the only truth. They follow blindly Hitler's leadership, which results in the present convulsion of the world.

Hitler's menace to the outside world is now being proven with disastrous effects, but his evil demeanor to his own people is not yet commonly admitted, and this still requires proof. These proofs are readily furnished by an examination of the conditions in Germany immediately preceding the outbreak of the war.

IN SATAN'S DOMAIN

IN *Mein Kampf* Hitler quite often refers to "Almighty" but never to "God" or "Christ." His "Almighty" is nothing but the symbol of a racial myth. His terminology in the religious realm constitutes the most deceptive camouflage of modern spiritual warfare. The extent to which this can reach is vividly illustrated by a recent harangue of Hitler's spiritual henchman Alfred Rosenberg on the occasion of the so-called consecration of an *Alltagskirche* (church for every day) with the usual pagan ceremonials. The theme of the address, curiously enough, was Martin Luther. Of him, he said, "We shall not falter in taking that great German (Martin Luther) to protect him from his own Lutherans and to announce that he belongs neither to creed nor to church but to the German people only." "*A new authority has arisen in Germany to say what are the meanings of Christ and Christianity. That authority is Adolf Hitler.*" This, of course, is the much vaunted "positive Christianity" which the Nazi party pledged itself to protect and promote. Those who know what is really meant see that this new faith will flourish and grow strong only when God-fearing Judaism and real Christianity — Catholic or Protestant — have been destroyed.

The central pressure is upon the unification of man's two highest mass emotions — loyalty to God and to race-state. When the one is absorbed completely into the other — and when the one to do the absorbing is the latter — there is placed in the hand of the political head of the State power over the conscience as well as over the civil liberties of every citizen from the smallest to the greatest.

Religious resistance to Hitler was therefore inevitable from the first. It would have been much greater had those involved been aware of the real situation confronting them. The camouflage of language did much to postpone the day of real disillusionment:

— 19 —

and it was intended to do just that. All religious resistance worthy of consideration — be it Catholic or Protestant — had had at least the following things in common: the conviction that God is greater than any man, even a Nazi dictator; that the philosophy of racialism, state absolutism, and pagan opportunism has no place in religion; and that the transferring of Nazi political ideals and methods into the realm of religion is unthinkable. Karl Barth, distinguished theologian, who was expelled from his Bonn University post and from the Reich soon after Hitler's rise, put it thus: "Nazi theory has no abiding place in the Church. If it prevails it will be the end of the Church. The fellowship of religion is not through blood and not through race. If the German Evangelical Church excludes the Jewish Scriptures or regards them as of secondary importance, it ceases to be the Church."

If, on the other hand, Nazi leaders let up on their drive to control the consciences and the character-forming processes of education of all Germans — which means the setting up of substitutes for existing religious movements in Germany, they will cease to be orthodox Nazis.

What is Hitler's position on Christianity? Let us note it to make plainer the reason for the course matters have taken under his leadership. In the first place he presents Nazism virtually as a new religion which consists in the deification of the German race — from the Nazi viewpoint: "God's decision has been made. The responsibility for the whole German people has been placed solely with the Fuehrer!" (Address given on Dec. 13, 1937.

In the second place Hitler clearly expresses the view that Christianity must either be changed into this new religion which "for the sake of clearness" (!) he calls "positive Christianity" — or else it must be destroyed by intolerance and terror. Here are his exact words on this subject taken from *Mein Kampf*: "Fanatical intolerance alone made it possible to build up that adamantine creed (Christianity); it is an absolutely essential condition of its existence. A world view animated by devilish intolerance can be broken only by a new conception impelled by a similar spirit and fought for with an equally strong will . . ; Force is broken only by force and terrorism only by terrorism."

The steady alienation of church property, particularly Roman Catholic property, has received occasional notice in the press. What it portends is clear enough to those who know the Nazis. It will not end until the great holdings of the churches — and probably of *all* the churches — have been transferred to the control of the party which teaches every youth, in its handbook that "Jews, Masons, and the churches, Catholic and Protestant" are the bitter enemies of the "race-blood-and-soil" basis of the Third Reich.

A pre-war A. P. dispatch from Germany announced "that the swastika and the flag of Adolf Hitler's black-shirted S. S. Elite Guards were raised ceremoniously over the Catholic archbishop's palace which was seized for use as S. S. headquarters. Friedrich Rainer, Nazi district leader, in a short speech declared the official taking possession 'denotes the disappearance of another figment of the churches' world power' and its return to the community.'"

Another A. P. dispatch, dated May 28, 1939, tells about the cessation in Germany of religious programs on the air, and that Bibles and religious tracts may no longer be displayed by booksellers. The dispatch tells the story, that devout Protestants and Catholics listen in vain for Whitsun religious programs on the air.

Inquiry disclosed that Germany had banned also radio broadcasts of religious services and that the Nazi government also was putting a curb on the sale of Bibles and church tracts.

Orders such as the radio ban are not published, but are transmitted secretly by the Propaganda Ministry to the government broadcasting administration. Examination of radio programs for the past four weeks indicated that radio sermons had disappeared unannounced. The radio, it was explained, is a government institution and the government is not a "confessional" or church instrument.

Church officials have urged that the broadcasts be resumed for the benefit of invalids and those who live far from churches, but their requests have fallen on deaf ears.

A new order of the Reich's Literary Chamber, an adjunct of the Propaganda Ministry, provides that Bibles and religious tracts may be put on display only in confessional book stores. In general book stores Bibles may be sold only when specifically ordered. There are few stores devoted solely to the sale of religious literature in Germany.

A further order by the chamber provides that Bible or tract societies no longer may subsidize book publishers, but that all religious publications must pay for themselves. Religious circles contend that publication of tracts usually is possible only because the publisher is subsidized by societies interested in the distribution of these tracts.

Reports reaching officials of the Protestant Confessional Synod also indicate that the State has declined to pay its customary subsidies to a considerable number of Lutheran and Evangelical ministers who have not wholeheartedly embraced Nazism. About fifty ministers in the Rhineland, fifteen in Silesia and twenty-five in Berlin and Brandenburg were said thus to have parts of their income cut off.

Nothing is being done in Germany without orders from above. What may those orders be? Here is another news item, that has reached us, dated Vienna, July 4, 1939:

"Theodor Cardinal Innitzer, Archbishop of Vienna, was brutally assaulted in Koenigsbrunn on Sunday following a series of Nazi demonstrations while he was making a tour of rural districts northwest of Vienna, it was learned today. He was pelted with rotten eggs and potatoes by a mob of rural Nazis, who shouted murderer and other epithets as he left a Koenigsbrunn church. His biretta (cap) was knocked off by a blow from a stick.

"In some villages, it appears, there were such demonstrations as bands of youths marching up and down whistling outside the churches where the Cardinal was celebrating mass. At another place a man tried to spit on the prelate as he passed, while women hissed and booed.

"Despite these demonstration Cardinal Innitzer continued his tour but always slept in the parish priests' houses. At one of them a number of windows were smashed during the night. Each visit was announced in advance by a placard on a church door.

"In one village twelve children were to have been confirmed in front of the church, but a threatening crowd gathered and the ceremony was held within the church."

Another indication of the debasement of Christianity in Germany is the story of Pastor Martin Niemoeller, who has been in German prisons more than two years. The whole story would take long to tell. Niemoeller was a submarine commander during the World War, then tried farming, and did manual labor while studying for the ministry. He was an early member of the Nazi party, breaking with Hitler when the Fuehrer attempted, through Bishop Mueller, to drum up the support of the Lutheran Church for the Nazi revolution. When Mueller, as Reich Bishop, ordered the churches into line, Niemoeller defied the order. For a time, so great was the antagonism stirred up by Nazi paganism among the rank and file of Lutherans, that Niemoeller seemed to have won a victory over Mueller and his successors. In 1937 Hitler felt strong enough to arrest him and to retain him in "protective custody" after a trial court had nominally set him free.

It is well known everywhere, that Pastor Niemoeller has no connection with the underground movements in Germany the object of which is to overthrow the Nazi government. He is certainly no Communist. From the record it would appear that he had no quarrel with the purely secular policies of the Nazis. He has simply taken his stand, as many Catholics have done, on the platform that in matters of private conscience "we must obey God rather than man." The great schism of Martin Luther's time does not divide the churches when a fundamental principle like this is at stake.

Should anybody have ever doubted Hitler's religious point of view, it is now made clear by Niemoeller's martyrdom. Nazism is itself a religion, which attempts by force to command the citizen's whole allegiance. It is necessarily intolerant of the Protestant and Catholic faiths as it is of the Jewish faith. It is necessarily at war with the ethical system which had its rise in the Hebrew prophets and reached one of its loftiest expressions in the Sermon on the Mount. It is, by its very nature, an enemy of the human conscience.

Pastor Niemoeller is not the only victim of Hitler's religious persecution. Thousands of others are undergoing torture in the Nazi concentration camps and prisons. One of them, Pastor Schneider of Dickenshied was murdered on July 18, 1939, after he was imprisoned for more than two years.

With Pastor Schneider's death the Confessional Church of Germany lost one of it most militant champions in its fight against State interference with the freedom of worship. One of the first and most emphatic objectors to State interference in spiritual affairs, Pastor Schneider early got into difficulties with the National Socialist authorities.

At the time of his death he had been in concentration camps longer than any other Confessional pastor, including Pastor Niemoeller. At first he was placed in a Rhineland concentration camp but later was moved to Buchenwald. near Weimar. which is reported to be the most severe of all Nationalist Socialist concentration camps.

Although the news of his death did not reach Berlin until a few days later a requiem service was held in Pastor Niemoeller's Dahlem Church.

The church was filled and the windows were opened so that those standing outside could hear the service conducted by Dr. Osterloh, substitute for the imprisoned Pastor Niemoeller. It began with the reading of a psalm.

The sermon, which avoided any hostile utterances, took for its text Mark xiii, 31.

At the conclusion the pastor made the unusual request that each member of the congregation should return home and read the entire thirteenth chapter of Mark and meditate it.

The Thirteenth Chapter of the Gospel according to St. Mark being symbolic to the state of affairs in Germany, we therefore, bring to the notice of our readers its following passages:

"And Jesus answering said unto him, Seest thou these great buildings? There shall not be left one stone upon another, that shall not be thrown down."

"And Jesus began to say, Take heed lest any man deceive you:

"For many shall come in My name, saying, I am Christ; and shall deceive many.

"And when ye shall hear of wars and rumors of wars, be ye not troubled; for such things must needs be; but the end shall not be yet.

"For nation shall rise up against nation, and kingdom against kingdom.

"For they shall deliver you up to councils; and in the synagogues ye shall be beaten: and ye shall be brought before rulers and kings for my sake, for a testimony against them.

"Now brother shall betray the other to death, and the father the son; and the children shall rise up against their parents, and shall cause them to be put to death.

"But when ye shall see the abomination of desolation, spoken of by Daniel the prophet, standing where it ought not (let him that readeth understand), then let them that be in Judea flee to the mountains;

"And let him that is on the housetop not go down into the house, neither enter therein, nor take anything out of his house.

"And if any man shall say to you, Lo, here is Christ; or, Lo, he is here; believe him not:

"For false Christs and false prophets shall rise, and shall show signs and wonders, to seduce, if it were possible, even the elect."

Who are the "false Christs and false prophets"? Their Satanic identity does not require additional proves. Nevertheless we will bring here a document which we have recently received from a correspondent in Germany.

The document is *The Official Guide for the Education of the Hitler Youth* (an organization which embraces all the German youth and is compulsory). The *Guide* contains fifty points, ten of which (we would say, the Ten Commandments of the devil) pertain directly to religion. They are as follows:

1. *Christianity is a religion for slaves and fools.*

2. Christianity and Communism are identical.

3. Christianity does not differentiate between white people and Negroes.

4. The New Testament is a Jewish lie by four evangelists.

5. The Church is international.

16. There is no Christian culture.

18. Christianity has spoiled the German people, because it has taught them ideas such as adultery and theft, which they had never known.

20. Christianity is only a substitute and cover for Judaism, and was invented by Jews in Rome.

21. Jesus Christ was a Jew.

24. How did Christ die? Whining on the cross. How did Planetta die? Shouting "Heil Hitler!" (Planetta was the murderer of Chancellor Dolfuss).

26. The Ten Commandments are a manifestation of the lowest instincts of humanity.

45. The new Eternal City is Nurenberg. Rome is doomed.

— 23 —

GERMAN WOMEN IN SLAVERY

Men of homosexual inclinations usually feel an aversion towards women. Hitler abhors them.

When he published *Mein Kampf* he must have been advised to be prudent and he omitted all passages relating to women. A women-opposition would surely have doomed his movement to failure. Only one paragraph was permitted to slip unnoticed and the genuine Hitler had yielded.

That paragraph refers to Hitler's notion on state construction. The subjects of the State he divided in two categories: *state citizens* and *state members. It must become a greater honor*, said he, *to be a street-cleaner and a "citizen" of the Reich than to be a king in a foreign state ... But the men without honor or character, the common criminal, the traitor to the Fatherland, etc., are to be deprived of that honor — they then become "state members."*

Then he added: *"The German girl is"* (like "the man without honor" and "common criminal") . . . *"a state member."*

Inasmuch as Hitler has exercised prudence towards women before he reached power, he became brutally frank when he began lawmaking in Germany. The German women were placed in a position of virtual slavery. They were denied all the privileges they have gained under the Weimar constitution and they were set back to the shameful status of real "state membership" in accord Hitler's evil conception. German women were put out of all political positions, their organizations suspended, a quota for women students in the universities established, and married women physicians and lawyers forbidden to practice. Every effort was begun to return women to the home, their own or another's, domestic service became compulsory to the unmarried women driven out of factory and office, that their places should be taken, by the Brown Shirts.

All this was in line with Hitler's feelings toward womankind and also with his avowed purpose to make Germany a militaristic nation. He needs many children to provide soldiers in plenty and also settlers for the conquered lands. The contributions women can make to such a state is as mothers or nurses, with the provision that they should also be workers in field and barn when the men are called away for military duty.

These "callings" for women do not require higher education — only a submissive spirit and a strong physique. Therefore the Nazis have completely reorganized the system of the girls' education. Although women are still permitted to attend universities, but their number is limited to a quota of only 10 per cent of the entire student body and the whole number of women-students is limited to 10,000. Some faculties, such as law and others, were closed to them entirely, while the number of women in medical schools has been limited to 75 for the entire Reich. For, conceived Hitler, *"the woman is needed at the bedside as much as the man at the gun."*

Conditions, however, have later of changed. Since more and more men have been enlisted in the army, women have been taken back to the factories, where they are required to work for meagre wages, and under most pitiful conditions.

In July, 1939, not less than 37% of all employed Germans were women—a higher percentage than the one attained in the United States, England, of France. At the same time there was a most deplorable discrepancy between male and female wages for the same kind of work. The hourly earnings of women run from 41 to 42.8 per cent lower than those of men. And, as always, the lower the wages drop the more the demand for women workers rose.

The encouragement of marriage, by loans to the couple, was not given unless the bride agreed not to accept work outside the home as long as the husband earned enough to keep him off relief. Child bearing was encouraged by the provision that with every living child born, one-quarter of the debt would be written off. However, the pressure of actual conditions has forced later on a modification of this decree. Loans have been granted even to the wives who did not resign from their jobs. Since 1933 over a million loans have been granted and 700,000 remissions made on the birth of a child. This is not a very brilliant record, less than one child per family in six years. Even trained by Hitler

Germans refuse to bear children as cannon fodder.

The general attitude towards women is that the importance of the home is of insignificance compared with the State. The tendency is to put the children more completely under outside authority and to interpose the State between them and their parents. Moreover, the outspoken lowly attitude towards women, the glorification of military virtue and the haughtiness towards such qualities which are peculiarly feminine, create a contemptuous feeling on the part of the boys towards their mothers.

Miriam Beard quoted Goebbels as having pronounced: "We Nazis have put women out of public life. Nature has fitted women for life behind the four walls of a house, not for life in the open. If she disputes the laws of life with man, he may become a house tyrant. She must cheerfully leave the education of her children to men who can prepare her sons so much better for heroic sacrifice upon battlefields."

THE PLIGHT OF GERMAN LABOR

When Hitler began, what he called, "his earthly career," he "scabbed" against his fellow workers. When, in January, 1933, he became the dictator of Germany, the destruction of the trade unions was the immediate objective of his control and this was accomplished forthwith. But the welding of a vise of autocratic control over labor was a long term job to be concocted by coercion and propaganda. The coercion was furnished by the state machinery. The propaganda was formulated by the Leader Principle, which means nothing less than that it is the police-enforced duty of the workers to do what they are told to do by the leaders.

To express and enforce the Leader

Principle among the rank of labor there was set up the Labor Front — a gigantic, nationwide *company union*. And in this most highly developed form of company-unionism, the employer is the "Leader" and the workers are the followers.

To quote the opening lines of the February, 1937, publication of the National Industrial Conference Board — research organization of American employers:

"The National-Socialist government does not believe in and does not permit collective bargaining in industry. It prohibits strikes and lockouts. It places in the hands of the employer, as leader, full responsibility for the maintenance of satisfactory working conditions in his establishment and vests him with the necessary authority. The employees, or followers, of the leader cannot refuse to abide by the decisions of the employers, but they can complain against them to the labor trustee who is an official of the government. The labor trustee is the court of first instance and last resort.

"Among the duties defined by law for the Labor Trustees is that of trying workers who through malicious agitation endanger labor peace within the shop, deliberately interfere with the management or make frivolous complaints to the labor trustees."

The semi-official Institute of Business Research has checked labor's balance sheet after about five years of Nazism in Germany and brought out a few outstanding facts:

1. Wages have been stabilized at or below the depression low levels. The index of average hourly wage rates for male, female, skilled and un-skilled labor declined from a monthly average of 86.2 in 1932 to 78.9 in June, 1939 — a drop of 2.7 per cent. The decline for skilled male workers was even greater — from 81.6 to 78.3 a total of 3.3 per cent. In connection with wage rates, it must be remembered that even the lowest wage was subject to taxes and deductions of one kind or another that at the most conservative- estimates amounted to, at least, 20 per cent.

2. The cost of living has increased. Food has been adulterated. The total index for the cost of living according to the aforementioned Institute, increased from 117.4 in January, 1933, to 134.8 in October, 1938 — an increase of 17.4 per cent. The increase for two of the three items constituting the bulk of the budget of workers — food, clothing, and shelter has been even greater. The food index increased from 107.3 in January, 1933, to 131.3 in October, 1938 — an in-

crease of 24 per cent. During the same period the index for clothing climbed from 112.4 to 127.2 — or 14.8 per cent.

3. Hours of work have been increased and a speed-up system instituted among workers. The increase in nominal wages as a result of increased hours is more than over balanced by the increase in the cost of living.

4. Trade unionism has been destroyed and its leaders murdered, exiled or placed in concentration camps.

In marked contrast on the other side of the picture is the following:

1. Concentration of industry into fewer hands. By September, 1938, the accumulated profits of private concerns were so great that the larger of them were expanding at the expense of the smaller. As an instance it was pointed out, that by that time the German Dye Trust controlled approximately half of the German chemical production as compared with one-third in 1933, and that Otto Wolff the Rheinish industrialist was buying up factories so rapidly that he began to give the impression of being another Hugo Stinnes."

Since the basis of the upswing in German production was armaments, the government as the largest buyer could hardly do other than patronize the biggest concerns and they received the cream of the business; they have been favored in the allotment of orders, raw materials and foreign exchange.

2. Profits have increased. "The earnings of industry as a whole," according to the Institute of Business Research, "— carefully estimated on the basis of balance sheet figures — increased from about 200 million R.M. in 1933, to about 1.9 billion R.M. in 1937." In addition to a profit of more than 5 per cent, some 1,500 stock companies representing half the total of German capital stock have been

to lay aside large sums for depreciation to make up for the years of depression.

These were the conditions in 1937. Later they were even worse. The Reichs-Kredit-Gesellschaft, a leading Berlin bank, issued its semi-annual survey of Germany's economic situation in July, 1939, from which we gather various points of increasing tension in the German economic system.

The first, is the increasing shortage of goods, which was attributed mainly to the fact that while total working income rose 64.2 per cent between 1933 and 1939, the production of consumption goods increased only 29.5 per cent.

A substantial share of the increase in the working income was collected by the State in increased taxes and levies, but the production of consumption goods still lagged far behind the increased purchasing power.

This was also evident from the fact that, while the production index of the "production goods" industries, which included armaments, rose from 45.7 in 1923 to 145.3 in April, 1939, the index of the consumption goods industries increased only from 74 in 932 to 112.8 in April, 1939.

To what extent the boom in Germany was a State-financed boom, or more exactly, a "cannon boom," was illustrated by the fact that of a total r 12,000,000,000 marks spent in building construction no less than 7,900,000,000 marks went for public "building," including military construction, 2,100,000,000 marks for industrial buildings, most of which were for the Four-Year Plan of economic armament, and only 2,000,000,000 for new housing.

Another point of tension lay in the lowering wage rates, which pressed against the fixed price structure. Despite the strict control, the minimum rates fixed by the State were valid in only a few industries, and that, in fact, the actual wage and income development has slipped from the hands of the State.

That was illustrated by the fact that, while the number of employed manual workers rose by 62.1 per cent between 1932 and 1939, their income rose not more than 64.2 per cent.

"A summary of the balance sheets of fifty of the most important German industrial corporations showed that the "cannon boom" has not been unprofitable to them. From 1936 to 1939, they increased the value of their plant from 2,524,000,000 to 3,792,-000,000 marks, their stock of supplies from 931,000,000 to 1,954,00,000 marks, their depreciation charges from 436,000,000 to 963,000,000 marks and their net profits from 251,000,000 to 1,804,000,000 marks.

In contrast, despite the special attention paid by the National Socialist regime to the German peasant, whose prices were raised immediately after Adolf Hitler came to power, German agriculture reported an annual deficit variously calculated between 4,300,-000,000 and 4,522,000,000 marks.

To eliminate this deficit, it was estimated, agricultural prices would have to be raised by another 40 per cent, which would have meant a further 15 per cent increase in the German living costs, which have already risen far beyond the less than 10 per cent shown by the official index figures.

As regards the cost of the "cannon boom" the survey remained discreet. It cited the increase in the Reich Government's tax revenues, which rose from 6,647,000,000 marks in 1932-1933 to 17,712,000,000 marks in 1938-39, with the income tax alone showing an increase of no less than 42.7 per cent last year, as compared with the preceding year. And it cited the official figures of the declared public debt, totaling 43,774,000,000 marks as of March 31, 1939, for Reich, State and communities.

But it was silent on the German "secret debt," which was variously estimated at between 20,000,000,000 and 25,000,000,000 marks, and which raised the total public debt upward of 64,000,000,000 marks, as compared with 24,300,000,000 marks in 1932.

As time passed the true picture of Nazism revealed itself in its nakedness, as a monopoly control of capitalist its most brutal expression. In face the picture presented even by the of cial figures, who would now da maintain that Nazism in German (the same as fascism in Italy) is something accidental? There certainly is no idealism in it. It is but a fiendish invention of the very few privileged reactionaries to keep in chains the overwhelming majority of the masses of the people.

DEPOSITION OF JUSTICE IN GERMANY

The following is a story of a workingman who underwent imprisonment in a Nazi Concentration Camp. This story is not unusual. In Germany there were, and there still are, hundreds of thousands of similar victims who were even more monstrously tortured for crimes they have never committed and for acts of which they were innocent.

The workingman was suspected of being implicated in Trade Unionist activities and was arrested by the Secret Police, who were anxious to obtain from him the name of another offender (whom, as it happens, he did not know). He suffered a beating, and then for several more weeks had his hands chained behind him during the day, and to the sides of his bed at night. Some of his friends suffered a worse degree of this treatment (which was also intended to force the giving ...ames); they were imprisoned in dark cells, their arms, in a half raised position, being chained to the wall behind them, and at night in bed their ankles were chained as well as their arms. Had the prisoners agreed to divulge the names of their old friends this torture at least would have been spared them.

Of his own beating the workingman, telling his story, made light. "It was not with *whips*" in his case. But he had a friend, a man of strong will and great powers of endurance, a man who had gone through the War and was well trained in its horrors. He was repeatedly flogged with whips and so mishandled that he felt his powers of resistance beginning to give way. Fearing he might lose his self-control and betray the names of his friends, he attempted to commit suicide. Even without suffering torture to this degree his friend felt that his morale had been shaken. "That is the worst part — the *Demoralisierung;* the effect of the chaining up, the humiliation and the gradual losses of confidence in oneself. A beating makes one angry, and it passes, but from the chaining there is no relief; one feels one's will power breaking down — that is the worst. And then the *solitude* in a tiny cell with absolutely nothing to do hour after hour, day after day, when one has been used to an active life! That in itself drives one almost mad. I had a pin in the lapel of my coat and I filled up some of my time by scratching patterns on scraps of paper. But when the guard saw what I was doing, *the pin was taken away."*

The workingman was a simple type of his class, steady and unemotional.

narrated the incident of the pin as a trifling one. But the picture seemed to bring in a flash some realization of pitiless exactness with which the colossal great new machine of the National Socialist State carries on its work, breaking the bodies and souls of all who dare to stand in its way, and grinding them to powder. The incident of the pin brings to one's mind the words of Herr Freisler (a high official in the Ministry of Justice), who wrote that "the aim of the Law must be not to combat the adversary but to annihilate him."

It is not sufficiently realized outside Germany that the Concentration Camps — the main means employed for the annihilation of adversaries or supposed adversaries — are an almost unprecedented institution in a country which has had an established legal system, for they are entirely outside the jurisdiction of the Law. They are not under the Ministry of Justice, and are controlled by the Secret Police, who may almost be said to constitute "A State within a State." Three years ago a special law was passed giving legal recognition to the State Secret Police as an independent branch of the Administration, and giving legal sanction to the powers already seized and to the practices already adopted. Even the heads of Provincial Governments must bow to the orders of the Gestapo.—This body, under the dictatorship of Herr Himmler, carries on its independent jurisdiction from which there is no appeal to courts of justice. It makes its own arrests, detains prisoners in the camps without trial for an indefinite period, and inflicts punishments, many of which amount to torture, such as flogging and the use of chains. The Commandants of the Camps are free to inflict the death sentence; death indeed often occurs without a "sentence," and is usually notified as

"death while trying to escape." Such are the plenary powers allowed to the Secret Police that men and women who have served sentences in prison, on their release are often carried off by the Secret Police and placed in a Camp. There are cases when they have never been heard of again. An inmate of a prison may hope at least for a trial — even if long delayed; and he can enlist the services of a lawyer, though it is hard indeed for the lawyer any longer to act as a really "free" agent.

Germany's Penal Code, moreover, has been recast. The principle of "no crime, no punishment" has disappeared, or rather the definition of "crime" has been stretched to cover the crimes of "intention" (whether action has followed or not). This passes easily into the crime of *opinion* in which an "intention" may be implied. It is not only with the object of wringing from them the names of other persons that prisoners are tortured in "examination prisons" and in Camps. There is also the object of forcing from them confessions of opinion in which, if they differ from the Nazi outlook, a criminal intention may be found to reside. The new German "law" gives every facility for convicting anyone guilty of holding such opinions, as judged by the final criterion of justice, the National Socialist view of life. In essence all crimes are reduced to an act of treason against the National Socialist State.

The Judge, once said Herr Hess, must give his judgment in accordance with the spirit and the history of a State. "There should be no abstract academical law which floats in the clouds." The law must be regarded by National Socialism as an active servant of the Community. The spirit of their State was in reality the spirit of the German people, and of this the Fuehrer was the incarnation. Herr Hess took for his text on this occasion a saying of Treitschke's, "The practice of law is a political activity." Herr Gurtner himself, the Minister of Justice, declared (at the Penal Congress, August, 1938) that the question of "guilt" is determined in the New Germany not only by the laws but also by "the sound feelings of the German nation." A judge is not to be bound by the written word, by the rigidity of legal definition; he may sentence a man for "any attack on the interests of the National Community," and in so doing he must act "according to a uniform view of life," given to the nation by National Socialism.

This "uniform view of life" includes a highly simplified ethical code. One can find a typical exposition of it in the National Socialist *Year-Book*, 1939. The maxim is laid down Party Members that "Right is whe advantageous to the National Soci Party." Till recently the more mon formulation of this basic p ciple ·has been that of Herr Frank Minister and Reich Jurist Leader: "Right is what serves the German people and the German race." The development is symptomatic. Right is not even that which (from a materialistic and short-sighted point of view) serves the interests of the people. The people themselves must now have no interests, no standards of conduct, no principles of justice, nor even of religion except in so far as they harmonize with what is laid down by the Party. "The National Socialist programme is your dogma" is another maxim in the *Year-book*.

IN CONCLUSION

Caesarism of old ruled by bread and circuses. Nazi-Caesarism invests the people's supply of bread in armaments and it serves the masters who accumulate fabulous wealth through scarcity /of others. "Circuses" are therefc e indispensable in order to distract and hypnotize the masses, to propagate intoleranpe, racial absurdity and other nonsense, to persuade the hungry that guns are preferable to bread and to deflect their resentment from their despots onto foreign "enemies" or domestic scapegoats: Jews, Marxists, and others.

Sometimes fiction endures. But when the victims of delusion ultimately discover themselves as greatly deceived and ground down into an unbearable position by their insane "leaders" and exploiters, when at last it dawns upon them that they are merely cannon fodder for the military machine they have unwittingly them selves created for their own destruction, then the day of reckoning will come. Then Germany will again be free.

The Nazi lie is now being exposed by a world disaster. At least the democratic forces in other lands have sincerely combined and are at present firmly resisting further Nazi aggression by a collective attack against it. The lie is being exposed amid universal desolation and death. Now may we pray that the German people will soon come to their senses and the iniquities of the Nazis will collapse within the Reich as a result of their own corruption, and eternal Peace and Righteousness will hereafter reign over the exhausted and suffering world.

Lightning Source UK Ltd.
Milton Keynes UK
UKHW022216310822
408150UK00013B/60